HINDU INDIA

FRONT COVER
A young, ash-smeared Shaivite sadhu, draped with prayer beads, bestows blessings during the Mahakumbh, 2001.

PAGE 1
Above: *The monkey god Hanuman, ardent devotee of Lord Rama.*
Below: *Garuda, the mythical half-bird, half-man, vehicle of Vishnu, the preserver.*

PAGES 2-3
A detail from the eleventh-century Lingaraja Temple in Bhuvneshwar, Orissa.

PAGE 4
The ritual spraying of water, mixed with turmeric, on Kallazhagar or Vishnu mounted on a golden horse, takes place during the Chitrai festival in Madurai, Tamil Nadu.

PAGES 6-7
Ritual offerings made to a silver tortoise embedded in the floor of the Brahma Temple in Pushkar, Rajasthan. Vishnu incarnated as tortoise to assist in the churning of the ocean of milk.

PAGES 8-9
Thousands of devotees take a ritual dip in the Ganges at Har Ki Pauri during the Kumbh Mela in Haridwar.

FIRST PUBLISHED BY BRIJBASI ART PRESS LTD. IN 2003

© **Text:** Devdutt Pattanaik
© **Photographs:** Individual photographers

Project Editor: Shalini Saran
Design: Anand Naorem
Published by: Brijbasi Art Press Ltd.
A-81, Sector V, Noida – 201301
Uttar Pradesh, India
email: brijbasi@bol.net.in
Website: www.brijbasiartpress.com

ISBN 81-87902-07-8

Processed and printed at Brijbasi Art Press Ltd.
E-46/11 Okhla Industrial Area, Phase II
New Delhi 110020

HINDU INDIA

by

Devdutt Pattanaik

BRIJBASI

Contents

8

Fountainhead

Where did it come from – this fantastic, mysterious, exciting, exotic, colourful, vibrant and enigmatic way of life known as Hinduism? Certainly not from a single source. No one book defines this religion of 700 million people. No single prophet has directed its destiny. It is an amalgamated vision of ancient seers, star-gazers, alchemists, philosophers, poets, priests, mendicants, farmers, traders, artisans, craftsmen, herdsmen, labourers and bards. It is manifested in a myriad narratives, symbols, rituals, hymns, customs and beliefs, and has evolved over 5000 years – sometimes like a tree, branching off with new ideas; sometimes like a river, coalescing from intellectual tributaries, yet always attempting to explain the meaning of and the means to cope with life.

Scripturally, the origins of Hinduism lie in the RigVeda, a collection of hymns or mantras dated philologically to c.1500 B.C. and astronomically to c. 5000 B.C. The word Veda means knowledge. Its mantras are believed to contain the secrets of the cosmos, revealed to seers known as rishis.

Manuals known as the Brahmanas dating to c.1000 B.C. offered instructions on how these chants could be used in an elaborate ritual known as a *yagna* during which offerings were made through fire to celestial beings, or devas, who, in turn, ensured the fertility of the land, the virility of men and the prosperity of the community.

That the *yagna* did not need a permanent shrine and that its altar was portable, suggest that the people who revered the Veda were most probably nomads. The glorification of war and the reverence for cows indicate that they were cattle-herding, chariot-riding, city-raiding warriors. They were in all probability patriarchal, for in the chants robust and randy male warrior-gods all but sideline female deities. They called themselves the Aryas – the noble ones.

Archaeologically, the origin of Hinduism has been traced to cities which date to c. 2500 B.C. These brick-built cities were located in and around

Facing page: While celebrating Janamashtmi or the birth of Lord Krishna, devotees clamber on each other to obtain a pot of cream hanging from a tree. This recalls Krishna's childhood prank of stealing butter, which earned him the name of Makhan Chor, *the one who steals butter.*

Above: *Charna, a kind of decoration made as part of the celebration of childbirth. The swastika is the ultimate auspicious symbol. The word is derived from* su asti, *which means, Let good things happen.*

Below: This nineteenth-century Tanjore painting defines the seven major chakras. Chakras are whorls of energy located in the energy field which surrounds the physical body. The vitality of these chakras, which can be seen clairvoyantly, reveal the state of an individual's physical, emotional and spiritual well-being.

Facing page: Ramanandis, devotees of Lord Rama, gathered in prayer in Ayodhya. The words Shri Ram are printed on their clothes.

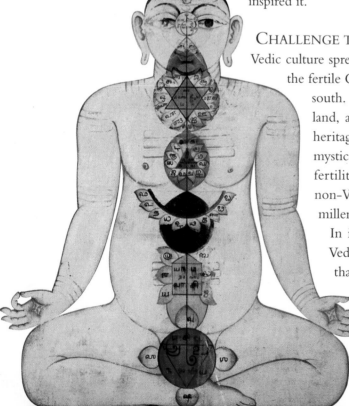

the valleys of the River Indus and the River Saraswati that once flowed majestically between the Indus and the Ganges through what is now the Thar desert. Nearly 1000 sites have been found, spread over 194,250,000 hectares.

The city dwellers were agriculturists, craftsmen and traders who had links with Mesopotamia and perhaps, even with Egypt. Their cities, characteristically utilitarian and devoid of ornamentation, were well laid out and efficiently maintained, suggesting the existence of a centralised government which was probably theocratic or plutocratic. Bitumen-layered roads criss-crossed the city to form a grid. There were bathhouses and granaries and even a sophisticated sewer system.

Though no temples have been identified, the icons, artefacts, amulets and seals found in these magnificent ruins display ritual imagery still found in the arts of rural India, suggesting the continuity of an unspoken tradition. Images evoking latter-day yogis and mother goddesses have been discovered, leading many scholars to conclude that several Hindu customs and beliefs, including phallic worship and adoration of the mother goddess, sprang from this silent culture.

The cities declined and disappeared around 1800 B.C. even as the Rig Veda was taking its final shape. The city-dwellers had a script. However, until it is deciphered we will never know for sure if the followers of the Veda overwhelmed the Indus-Saraswati civilisation, inherited it, or indeed, inspired it.

CHALLENGE TO VEDIC CULTURE

Vedic culture spread from the north-west of India to the east, down the fertile Gangetic plain. It also spread from the north to the south. In time, it became the dominant culture of the land, accommodating – not overwhelming – parochial heritage. Hence, beneath the overarching framework of mystical Vedic ideas, Hinduism contains a whole range of fertility rites and folk beliefs whose origins are non-Vedic. The process of assimilation continued over a millennium, from 800 B.C. to A.D. 800.

In its early days, sacrificial and priestly rituals of the Veda so dominated Hinduism that scholars identify that period as the Vedic Age. It witnessed the rise of Brahminism, a process by which Brahmins, or priests came to dominate Hindu society. They

consolidated and retained this position both ritually and socially in the centuries that followed.

By 800 B.C. there was a growing restlessness against Vedic ritualism and Brahminical orthodoxy. Society leaned towards mystical contemplation and esoteric speculation. The movement took two forms. On the one hand, warriors and priests turned into philosophers and sought the true nature of reality within the Vedas. On the other, there were monks or *shramanas* who sought the meaning of life outside the Vedic fold. The former were known as *astikas* or believers. The latter were the *nastikas* or non-believers. The *astikas* were theistic, identifying, adoring and sought union with the still and serene divine spirit that underlies all realities. The *nastikas* were atheistic or agnostic, seeking a way of life that liberated one from earthly woes. From the *astikas* came mystical discourses which later came to be known collectively as the *Upanishads* or Vedanta, the acme of the Veda. From among the *nastikas* rose two monastic orders known as Jainism and Buddhism, whose popularity threatened the very existence of Hinduism.

To begin with, Buddhism and Jainism were not ritualistic. They reached out to the masses and spoke the language of the people, which was Prakrit. They dealt with issues such as change and suffering that mattered to the masses, and displayed no interest in communicating with celestial beings. They would surely have overwhelmed Hinduism, had elitist Vedism not adapted itself and accommodated its ideology and philosophy to the beliefs and customs of the common man. In the process, classical Hinduism was born.

EMERGENCE OF CLASSICAL HINDUISM

Classical Hinduism fired the imagination of the people. Unlike Buddhism and Jainism, it did not see monasticism as the highest way of life. Nor did it frown upon theism. In fact, it celebrated the idea of the divine. Through tales chronicled in the *Itihasas* and the *Puranas*, dated between 300 B.C. and A.D.1500, divinity adopted a tangible form known as Bhagvan, the ultimate manifestation of the Godhead, or Parameshwar, supreme lord of all beings, devotion to whom solved life's problems. While Buddhism and Jainism based their beliefs on the laws of the cosmos, Bhagvan was seen as the cause and manifestation of the cosmos itself.

14

Above: The legend of Kaveri. Facing page: This Naga stone is from Assate, in Aurangabad district. Nagas, snakes, are revered as guardians of fertility, and their images are commonly worshipped throughout rural India.

Vedic priests appropriated non-Vedic liturgical texts known as the *Agamas*, causing the sacrificial *yagna* to give way to rituals of adoration known as puja, through which devotion for the Godhead was expressed. Grand temples were built in honour of various manifestations of Bhagvan: there was the world-affirming Vishnu, the world-renouncing Shiva and the world-embodying Devi.

Hinduism endeared itself to the laity by identifying village gods, guardian spirits, ancestors, saints and heroes, including Buddhist and Jain teachers, with Bhagvan. Political support was gained by projecting kings as representatives of the divine power, with a duty to institute and maintain divine laws on earth. Economic favour was gained by using fertility symbols; household rituals, aimed at harnessing the benevolent power of the cosmos, became part of mainstream life as mystical meanings were superimposed on them. Tantra, with its energy-transforming occult rites, and yoga with its psycho-physical alchemical practices, were no longer held in disdain. In fact they were commonly accepted, albeit in less complex forms.

In some parts of India, especially the south, where the northern Sanskrit tradition had mingled and merged with southern Tamil tradition, opposition to Buddhism and Jainism was occasionally violent. By A.D. 800, Buddhism was waning from the Indian landscape, Jainism had been successfully sidelined and classical Hinduism – accommodating priestly philosophy as well as lay beliefs – had pushed its way to the forefront. It was patronised by many royal families including the Guptas of Magadha, the Chalukyas and Rashtrakutas of the Deccan, the Pallavas and Cholas of Tamil Nadu, the Palas of Bengal and the Kesaris of Orissa.

The most powerful aspect of Hinduism that ensured its cultural domination over the subcontinent was the Bhakti movement which prescribed total surrender to the divine (perceived in the image of local gods) as the means to attain all goals. The movement inspired vibrant epics, legends, lyrics, music, theatre, rituals and more importantly, an egalitarian world view, which ensured its rapid transmission to every corner of India – from Tamil Nadu to Kashmir and from Maharashtra to Assam.

20

16-17
This grand procession of richly caparisoned elephants takes place near the temple in Trichur, Kerala, during Pooram.

PAGES 18-19
A detail from the Sun Temple at Konark, Orissa.

IMMIGRATION AND INVASIONS

Over the centuries, India has had its share of invaders and immigrants – Persians, Greeks, Scythians, Parthians, Huns, Gujars and other tribes from Central Asia – who mostly entered the country from the north-west. They brought with them ideas that enriched Hinduism, such as sun worship and the solar zodiac. They introduced the practice of wearing stitched clothes, mingled with the indigenous population, and in later centuries, some, like the Rajputs, became defenders of the Hindu faith in north India.

With the exception of Islam, Hinduism managed to assimilate all the cultures it came into contact with. Islam had a history of overwhelming the culture of the land it spread to, as had happened in Persia and Mesopotamia. But in India, things were different. Neither was Hinduism overwhelmed, nor was Islam assimilated. The two religions ended up coexisting, though not always peacefully.

Islam came into India a thousand years ago. It came peacefully with Arab traders whose ships frequented the ports on the west coast of India, and violently with Central Asian Turkish war-lords whose armies swept across the subcontinent from the north-west frontier to plunder the fabled wealth of Hind, the Arabic word for the land beyond the river known to the natives as Sindhu and to the Greeks as Indus.

The arrival of Islam shook the very foundations of Hinduism. Temples were demolished, idols broken, cities plundered, communities enslaved, women veiled and people converted as great Muslim empires were established in India. Eventually, an equilibrium was reached. In villages, Muslims lived in harmony with Hindu communities, participating in village festivals and fairs. In many places, there were converts, but caste rules were still upheld. Muslim rulers, like the Mughals of Delhi and the

Shahs of the Deccan, patronised Hindu scholars and married Hindu women. There was tremendous interaction between Hinduism and Islam. The Sufi mystics found much in common with the Bhakti movement of Hindu saints. To poet-saints like Kabir, the Hindu Rama and the Muslim Rahim were merely different words for the same divine principle. In the south, temples of warrior-gods and mother goddesses often had Muslim door-keepers and guardians. Hindus seeking divine favour frequented dargahs or shrines of Muslim saints. Bardic poetry came to be populated with heroes who were Muslim in some versions and Hindu in others.

The relationship between the Hindus and Muslims soured with the 'divide and rule' policies of the British Raj. Matters reached a climax during the Partition of India, when Pakistan came into being on grounds of religious incompatibility.

Europeans came to India by sea at the beginning of the sixteenth century, first as traders and then later as administrators. With them came Catholic missionaries, though Christianity itself had already come to India nearly 1500 years earlier when the apostle Thomas had arrived, probably with Roman or Arab traders.

By the end of the nineteenth century the British, and to some extent, the French, Portuguese and Dutch had established themselves as the rulers of the Indian subcontinent. Unlike the Muslim rulers, the Europeans kept a distance from their subjects. There was a conscious attempt to study the natives, not assimilate with them.

The result was the introduction of Hindooism in European universities and the Western media, as translators, anthropologists, sociologists, artists, philosophers, missionaries, reporters, travellers and theologians descended upon India. Some were impressed by the literary and philosophical traditions of the country. Others focused on everything that confirmed the belief that the native was a pagan savage. And then there were those who were spellbound by all that satisfied their craving for the exotic.

The word Hindu came into being only in the nineteenth century after Europe 'discovered' India. Initially, the word referred to the non-Islamic Hindi-speaking men of north India. Later it referred to that Indian religion which was not Islamic, Christian, Buddhist, Jain or Sikh. Creation of the word

21

Left: Exquisite leather puppets are made in Andhra Pradesh. The themes, chosen by puppeteers are mostly related to the epics. This is an image of Ravana, the ten-headed demon king of Lanka and a central figure in the epic Ramayana.

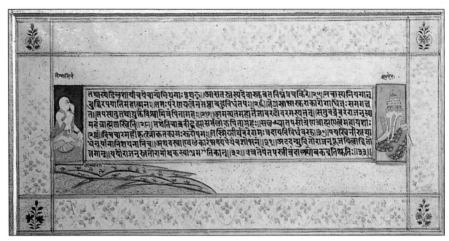

Hindu was necessary for both academic and administrative documentation. It rapidly became a popular tool of self-identification, even amongst the natives.

The European rulers introduced Western education to India, exposing Indians to scientific thinking and egalitarian political philosophies. The interest in Indian scriptures, their translations and subsequent publications that were once accessible only to a few, were now made available to all, including the lay Hindu. The result was an explosion of information and its reinterpretation.

Most of the early students were men from upper-class, high-caste families. From among these men rose the earliest Hindu reformers, such as Raja Ram Mohan Roy, who sought to bring out what was best in Hinduism, especially its philosophy and metaphysics; and stamp out the worst, including practices such as sati, or the burning of widows, child marriage and caste hierarchy. This was the great Hindu renaissance and reformation of the nineteenth century.

The twentieth century saw the rise of two forms of Hinduism: one apologetic, the other defensive. The former tried hard to distance itself from certain aspects of Hinduism, such as the caste system, idol worship and erotic temple sculptures, deeming them as latter-day corruption, and sanitising them through the lofty philosophies of the *Upanishads*. The latter justified and rationalised all Hindu practices, sometimes even challenging the traditional conclusions of historians, calling any attempt to criticise any aspect of Hinduism as the work of vested alien interests.

Thus, like its origins, the true nature of Hinduism remains ambiguous even amongst Hindus. What is undeniable though is that this way of life continues to metamorphose with time and space, responding to history, offering a dynamic and organic world view that makes the inevitable more palatable, inspiring all to appreciate the immediate, while offering glorious visions of what lies beyond.

Above: This elegant medieval manuscript on parchment deals with the subject of alchemy. Courtesy, National Museum, New Delhi.

Facing Page: *The vertical caste mark on the forehead indicates that the devotee is a follower of Vishnu. The names of Lord Rama and his consort Sita are also written on the woman's forehead.*

PAGE 24 AND BACK COVER
This 72-year-old man is in a deep trance as he is pierced with spikes as part of a ritual of mortification which takes place in Tamil Nadu.

Beliefs

To understand Hinduism, it must first be differentiated from the Abrahamic religions – namely Judaism, Christianity and Islam. Abrahamic religions are based on the paradigm of Original Sin, Fall of Man and the achievement of Redemption by following the path of God revealed through a chosen man – Moses, Jesus or Mohammed; and recorded in a book – the *Tanakh,* the Bible or the Koran, respectively. These ideas of Original Sin and Redemption are alien to the Hindu world view.

KARMA, DHARMA, MOKSHA AND YOGA

In Hinduism, life is not the result of any transgression. Events are determined by past actions, performed either in this lifetime or the one before. This is the law of karma. Both action and its reaction make up karma. It is believed that we have no control over events but can choose our reaction to these events. Thus, life is a manifestation of both fate and the human will.

The karma which has a favourable reaction is known as *punya*, while the karma which has an unfavourable reaction is known as *paap*. Worldly Hindus try hard to earn merit through *punya* and savour the joyful results. Karma is *punya* if it aligns itself with dharma.

Dharma refers to the divine code of conduct that ensures cosmic and social stability. It ensures action that bridles desire and motivates us to carry out our duties which are decided by our station and stage

Above: Floral offerings made at the feet of Lord Rama at a temple in Haridwar.
Right: The dancer, Leela Samson, performing the Surya Namaskaar, *the yogic salutation to the sun. The* Surya Namaskaar *comprises a range of movements and postures. The beneficial effects include physical well-being and mental equipoise.*

Facing Page: Muniyappan, a guardian deity on the banks of the Kaveri at Mattur Dam. The deity is especially propitiated for prosperity and abundant rain on the eighteenth day of the Tamil month of Adi.

Below: A man dressed as the monkey-god, Hanuman, ready to play his role in the Ramlila. Over the course of ten nights, the major events of the epic Ramayana are re-enacted in the. Ramlila, which takes place in almost every town and village in India.

in life. The word dharma is also used as a synonym for religion. True Hindus are those who follow the path of dharma. In fact, Hindus do not address their religion merely as Hinduism, but *sanatana dharma*, the eternal path.

Since every event in the Hindu scheme of things is a reaction, birth is also a reaction – to death and to actions in past lives. Karma ensures that we move from one lifetime to another, experiencing all the reactions of our former actions. Freedom from this merry-go-round of birth and death called *samsara*, is known as moksha or liberation. Moksha is the ultimate aim of Hinduism.

Yoga is the technique by which we can attain moksha. Simply put, yoga is the means to discipline the mind so that we recognise the true nature of existence and realise the divine within us. The approach may be intellectual (*gyan* yoga), emotional (bhakti yoga), physical (hatha yoga), a combination of these (*raja* yoga), or ritualistic (*laya* or tantra yoga).

GOD AND THE GODHEAD

The Hindu concept of god is complex. What makes it more so are the agnostic hymns that appear in some scriptures, such as the Nasadiya in the Rig Veda, that speculates on the origin of the universe: *Who knows what existed first, before creation? Even the gods came later.*

During Hindu rituals, a number of gods are invoked. First, there is Ganapati, the elephant-headed, pot-bellied remover of obstacles. Then there are the *ishta devata*, the personal god; the *kula devata* or family god; the *griha devata* or household god; and the *grama devata* or village god. These are followed by the devas, gods personifying natural phenomena. They can be terrestrial, like Agni, the fire-god; atmospheric, like Vayu, the wind-god; and celestial, like Indra, the rain-god. Then there are the *diggapalas*, lords of space and guardians of the ten directions, followed by the *navagrahas*, gods of time and guardians of the nine celestial bodies. Hindus also worship nagas, or serpent-gods, who are guardians of fertility.

Hindu gods are associated with, and exist in animal and plant life, and in the mineral kingdom. Thus cows, bulls, elephants and turtles are worshipped. Offerings are made to the banyan and pipal trees and the *tulsi*, or basil plant. Natural rock formations such as the Amarnath cave in Uttaranchal, mountain peaks such as Mount Kailas in Tibet, rivers like the Ganges and the Narmada, and lakes such as Mansarovar and Pushkar are revered. Ancestors who live in the land of the dead and await rebirth are also revered.

To Hindus, the whole world is a manifestation

PAGES 28-29
Durga, the 10-armed goddess of war, descends to earth to destroy evil. Elaborate images of her are worshipped for nine days and nights. On the tenth day, the image is taken out in procession and immersed in water. The worship of Durga coincides with the Ramlila.

PAGES 30-31
Kerala's most dramatic dance form, Kathakali, involves the use of elaborate costumes and make-up which takes several hours to apply. Krishna Attam, or the Dance of Krishna seen here, is as much an act of worship as it is of entertainment.

of the divine. There is no differentiation between the creator and creation. The world is an expression of divinity. Faith in Bhagvan guarantees liberation, for He alone can overturn the decree of karma. His will overrides all.

Bhagvan or the Godhead is visualised in different ways. The Vaishnavas view Him as Vishnu who incarnates on earth from time to time to restore order. The two most popular incarnations of Vishnu are Rama, the perfect king; and Krishna, the wise, wily and winsome cowherd. The Shaivas regard the ascetic Shiva as Godhead personified. While Vishnu is depicted as the world-affirming cosmic king, dressed in silk and gold and adorned with flowers and sandal paste, Shiva is the world-rejecting cosmic hermit, dressed in animal skins and smeared with ash. Vishnu celebrates the world of name and form; Shiva perceives it as a delusion of the unenlightened mind. Some Vaishnavas prefer directing their devotion to Vishnu through his servant, the monkey-hero Hanuman. Likewise, some Shaivas, especially in the south, prefer to reach Shiva through his son Murugan or Ayyappa.

The Godhead in Hinduism also manifests in a female form. Every village in India has its own goddess, embodying the spirit of the village. Addressed simply as Ma or Mata or Amma, which mean Mother, she is worshipped to ensure the fertility of the land and appeased to avert drought and disease. All village goddesses are considered to be manifestations of the supreme mother goddess Devi, which simply means goddess. Devi represents the material half of the cosmos while Shiva and Vishnu represent the spiritual half. They are two halves of the ultimate divine, complementary and totally interdependent.

Devi is worshipped in many forms including Lakshmi, goddess of abundance and good fortune; Saraswati, serene goddess of learning and the arts; Durga, the invincible warrior-maiden; Gauri, gentle goddess of the household; Kali, fierce goddess of the wilderness, and Bhagavati or Lalita Tripurasundari, the supreme manifestation of material reality. Devi is the tangible energy or Shakti of which the universe is made and which activates the potential within Shiva. Vishnu and Shiva personify the atman or intangible soul. Thus in Hinduism, matter is as much a manifestation of the divine as the spirit.

The Godhead is also worshipped through a number of parochial deities, such as Vithoba of Maharashtra who is identified with Krishna; Mallana of Karnataka who is seen as a form of Shiva, and the deity at Ahobilam in Andhra Pradesh who is visualised as Narasimha — the half-man, half-lion incarnation of Vishnu.

In the *Upanishads*, the divine is neither male nor female, neither animal nor plant nor mineral, neither parochial nor national. Divinity is seen as beyond form – the omnipresent and omnipotent principle which is changeless, unaffected by time or space, and which can be defined only by negation: not this, not that. It is both the cause and manifestation of the universe, but is itself without cause and beyond manifestation. This principle is termed as Brahman. It is characterised by *sat-chitta-ananda*, which means absolute truth, pure consciousness and perfect bliss.

THE ABSENCE OF EVIL

The word 'evil' has no synonym in any Indian language. It is of Judeo-Christian-Islamic origin and means devoid of divinity. This concept is contrary to the Hindu belief that everything is a manifestation of the divine. In the *Bhagavad Gita*, Krishna displays his cosmic form in which Arjuna is horrified to find not just creative forces, but destructive forces too. Friends, foes, heroes and villains all ultimately emanate from and assimilate into the divine.

Negative events and bad people are explained away by using the law of karma. Bad things happen due to *paap* or sin. Villains, murderers, rapists, enemies, marauders, thieves – they all exist because of *paap*. We are exposed to and affected by their misdemeanours because we are obliged to endure the repercussions of past misdeeds. The only way to ensure that our life is full of positive events, good things and good people is by accumulating *punya* and by atoning for past *paap*.

In the *Itihasas* and *Puranas* which chronicle Hindu myths, there is no equivalent of Satan. But there are many characters who may be perceived as demonic. There are the asuras who fight the gods, the *rakshasas* who harass humans, and the *pisachas* who annoy ancestors. None of them are seen as evil. They, too, are manifestations of the Godhead. They dwell in different planes of existence and their presence is necessary for cosmic balance.

The asuras live under the ground; they are the lords of material wealth belonging to the plant and mineral kingdoms, whom the devas, or gods of the celestial realm, have to overpower in battle in order to ensure that the world has an adequate supply of food and metal. Thus, it is not surprising that the harvest festivals of Dussehra, Diwali and Onam are associated with the triumph of the devas over the asuras or with the arrival of asura-kings such as Mahabali. *Rakshasas* are barbarians who live by the law of the jungle and are crushed by *manava*-kings (*manava* refers to the descendants of Manu, the first human). The prime example of a *manava* is Rama who established the code of civilisation or dharma. The *pisachas* are the dead who have not received proper funeral rites and who therefore cannot make their journey to the next life. Until they are appeased, they trouble the living and the dead.

Below: On Dussehra, the culmination of the Ramlila, giant effigies of Ravana, the demon king of Lanka, are set alight with crackers. Each locality has it own effigy, the burning of which celebrates the victory of good over evil and attracts thousands of visitors.

33

PAGES 34-35
The Chitrai festival of Tamil Nadu takes place in April/May. Kallazhagar (Vishnu) sets out from Alagerkoil to perform his sister Meenakshi's wedding at Madurai. This mission remains unfulfilled, and on his return he enters the Ramaraya mandapa where thousands of devotees spray a mixture of turmeric and water upon him.

PAGES 36-37
Thiruvarur is famous for its Thyagesa temple and magnificent chariot. When adorned, the chariot weighs 300 tonnes. During the festival this chariot, drawn by ropes made from the husk of 100,000 coconuts, is taken out in procession.

Facing Page: The harvest festival of Pongal takes place in mid-January. The second day of this festival is important, for it marks the onset of the sun's northerly course. The milk is boiled in a decorated metal or earthen pot tied with a stalk of turmeric. Jaggery, clarified butter and the newly harvested rice are then added. Pongal, rice pudding, is a special treat of this festival.

Gnomes and goblins known as *yakshas, ganas* and *pramathas* often surround Shiva. Devi has for her handmaidens fearsome and bloodthirsty women known as *yoginis, matrikas* and *mahavidyas.* They represent nature's wild, malevolent and dark forces, which are rejected by all except the divine. They are worshipped by people following the antinomian path of tantra that seeks to realise the Truth by facing suppressed realities, rather than sublimating them.

CLASSICAL AND FOLK TRADITIONS

Hinduism oscillates between the erudite metaphysics of priests and the practices of the common man. This has led commentators to conclude that Hinduism has an overarching classical framework dominated by Vedic texts and Brahminical ideology. Within this are numerous parochial customs and folk traditions.

The classical or *margi* tradition is supported by scriptures, primarily the Vedas, which are composed of *Mantra Samhitas* (compilation of hymns), Brahmanas (*yagna* manuals) and *Aranyaka-Upanishads* (metaphysical discourses). There are four *Mantra Samhitas:* Rig, Sama, Yajur and Atharva. These texts, especially the Rig *Mantra Samhita,* are regarded as *shruti,* or revelations of non-human origin. Then there are the smriti texts, or traditions of human origin. These include the *shastras,* or codes of conduct; *Itihasa-Puranas,* or myths, epics and legends; sutras, or philosophical aphorisms, and *bhasyas* or philosophical commentaries. Finally, there are the *agamas* or theistic liturgy, and many other temple and ritual texts.

Folk or *desi* tradition, while acknowledging divine revelation and human traditions, tilts more towards household and communal rituals. The focus is on practice rather than on belief. There is a greater emphasis on the immediate environment – earth, rain, fire, disease and death – and less on the soul, the afterlife and the nature of reality.

Classical Hinduism is dominated by Brahminical ideology, Vedantic speculation and grand temple traditions. Folk Hinduism is strongly influenced by alchemical and energy-transmutating tantric rites. It is concerned with the welfare of the village and the household, and the fertility of the land and women, and rarely involves priests. Classical Hinduism tends to be more monastic and views the world as maya, or the ephemeral delusion of the unenlightened mind. Folk Hinduism is more worldly, preferring to view earth and Nature as manifestations of energy or Shakti, embodied in a goddess.

Anthropological studies indicate that the classical has over time, appropriated and overwhelmed folk traditions, so that what was once a folk tradition is today classical. Likewise, what was once purely classical is now an

39

integral part of folk belief and practice. Assimilation and appropriation have been a two-way process.

BHAKTI AND VEDANTA

The most dominant belief in popular Hinduism today is bhakti, which means unconditional devotion to the divine. The concept of bhakti emerged in south India in the early centuries of the Christian era and rapidly spread across the country.

It began with the passionate songs of Shaiva and Vaishnava poet-saints known as Nayanars and Alvars, respectively. These songs inspired the masses to move away from blind Brahminical ritualism and submit to the will of the divine. Bhakti rapidly became a pan-Indian phenomenon between A.D.1000 and 1500.

Bhakti acquired a metaphysical foundation in Vedanta. According to Vedanta, empirical reality is a delusion. What is real and eternal is the atman or soul. The aim of Vedanta is to help the individual discover his soul – the *jiva-atman*, and through this discovery, realise the soul of the divine – the *param-atman*. Although there are many methods to make this discovery, and thus attain moksha, the simplest is bhakti. Vedanta schools can be broadly divided into two groups: the *Advaita* or monastic school according to which the *jiva-atman* is no different to the *param-atman*, and the *Dvaita* or dualistic school according to which the *jiva-atman* and the *param-atman* are distinct.

Vedic philosophy reached the masses through epics that concretised abstract metaphysical ideas through their characters and plots. The most popular among these epics are the Ramayana, the story of Rama; the *Shrimad Bhagavatam*, comprising the tales of Vishnu, especially in the form of Krishna; the *Shiva Purana*, or Shiva's chronicles; and the *Devi Mahatmya*, or the glory of the goddess. These were first written in Sanskrit but became truly accessible only when saints such as Kamban of Tamil Nadu and Shankar Dev of Assam rewrote and retold them in the vernacular.

PAGES 40-41
Offerings made by pilgrims to the river Ganges in Varanasi.

Facing page: *A monkey clambers up a temple wall and pauses as it confronts an image of the monkey god, Hanuman.*
Below: *This simian companion seems no burden for this sadhu to shoulder. Both have travelled from Bihar to the Pashupatinath Temple, Nepal.*

43

PAGES 44-45
The Karagam dance is performed balancing a pot on the head. The dancers are part of the victory procession of the Mysore Dussehra during which an idol of the goddess Chamundeshwari is placed in a golden howdah on the royal elephant.

PAGES 46-47
Naked Naga sadhus returning from a dip in the Ganges during the Kumbh. Hoardes of Naga sadhus are usually the first to enter the water on the auspicious bathing days which mark the month-long Kumbh Mela.

Below: *The elephant-headed god Ganesha is also worshipped as the scribe who wrote down the epic Mahabharat as it was being composed and recited by the sage Vyas. The Mahabharat is said to contain the wisdom of the Vedas.*

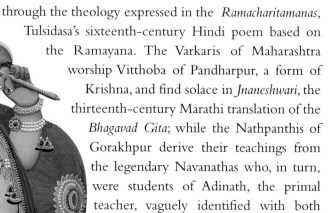

Though Vedanta philosophers like Shankara, Ramanuja, Madhava, Chaitanya and Vallabha were all Brahmins, the Bhakti movement itself characteristically rejected barriers of caste and gender. Some of the greatest inspirations of the movement came from women like Meera of Rajasthan and Lalleshwari of Kashmir; and men like Namdev, the tailor from Maharashtra; and Kanakadasa, a shepherd from Karnataka, both of whom belonged to lower castes. Instead of rituals, scriptures or philosophical commentaries, there lay at the heart of the movement, simple yet profound and passionate songs written in the language of the masses.

HOLY MEN AND THEIR ORDERS

Hinduism never was, and still is not, defined by a homogenous group. It has always been a collection of innumerable *sampradayas* or communities and *paramparas* or traditions. All the communities are united as Hindus by their common belief in the Vedas, and ideas such as karma, dharma, moksha and yoga. But each one is unique with its own personal god, guru or philosophy that gives the followers standards and codes of conduct to determine their destiny. Thus, the Ramanandis of Ayodhya visualise the divine as Rama and aspire to reach him as a servant does a master, through the theology expressed in the *Ramacharitamanas*, Tulsidasa's sixteenth-century Hindi poem based on the Ramayana. The Varkaris of Maharashtra worship Vitthoba of Pandharpur, a form of Krishna, and find solace in *Jnaneshwari*, the thirteenth-century Marathi translation of the *Bhagavad Gita*; while the Nathpanthis of Gorakhpur derive their teachings from the legendary Navanathas who, in turn, were students of Adinath, the primal teacher, vaguely identified with both Shiva and Vishnu.

Entry into most communities and traditions is by birth and determined by caste. But there have been communities where entry is through initiation. The ISKCON movement which is grounded in the Gaudiya Vaishanava tradition, is a case in point. Some, like the Lingayat and

Virashaiva communities in Karnataka, began as social reform movements in medieval times and have gradually transformed into hereditary communities.

New orders come into being each day. Some survive, others die out. The twentieth century saw the rise of gurus such as Swami Sivananda and Swami Muktananda through whose guidance many have found access to the divine. Indeed, some of these gurus such as Sathya Sai Baba and Amritanandamayi Amma have been given the status of godhead, for their wisdom has transformed them into the most potent vehicles of godly aura: the closest tangible experience man can possibly have of the divine.

Left: This image depicts Lord Vishnu in his incarnation as Rama, Ramaswamy Temple, Kumbakonam, Tamil Nadu.

49

PAGES 50–51
Hundreds of drummers and musicians add to the pageantry of the procession of elephants during the Trichur Pooram, Kerala.

PAGES 52–53
A devotee pays obeisance to the image of a guardian deity by a riverside.

PAGE 54
Rajasthani women make ritual offerings of flowers and water to Nandi, the bull, in the courtyard of a Shiva temple. The bull is the vehicle of Lord Shiva.

Practices

A Hindu is characterised less by what he believes in and more by what he does. There is a ritual to mark every occasion. It may be a communal obligation, a way to earn merit, or the means to ward off the undesirable. Whatever the reason, a ritual connects the individual with his community, his environment, the cosmos and the divine. It also influences his destiny.

Simple or elaborate, scriptural or popular, personal, domestic, social or associated with the temple, rituals vary from place to place and change with the times. Many ancient elaborate invocations have today been abbreviated to accommodate the fast pace of modern life.

Human birth indebts the Hindu to sages, gods and ancestors. The only way to repay this three-fold debt is by performing rituals: *yagna* for the sages, puja for the gods, and *samskara* for the ancestors. For the individual and his family, there is the *vrata* or personal observance.

Yagna is the earliest recorded Hindu ritual. The guidelines for this fire-sacrifice were put down over 4000 years ago in the Yajur Veda, the Brahmanas and in the *Griha* and *Srauta* sutras. Specially trained priests would prepare an elaborate altar, light a fire, invoke the devas through the power of mantras and offer them gifts, in the hope of gaining divine favour and worldly joy. A *yagna* could be a simple domestic ritual or a complex communal affair involving hundreds of priests and continuing for as long as ten years. Today, the *yagna* is no longer popular. It exists in an abbreviated form: the *homa* or *havan*, which is performed during a number of domestic and temple rituals. In many places, the reading and understanding of Vedic philosophy is considered the ideal substitute for the mechanical performance of the *yagna*.

The *yagna* has been sidelined by the puja, which is now a part of mainstream Hinduism due to the rising popularity of bhakti. In its essence, puja means ritualistic adoration of the divine. It may be a simple rite performed

Another image of Nandi. The word Nandi stems from Ananda, *which means the bliss of beings without desire.*

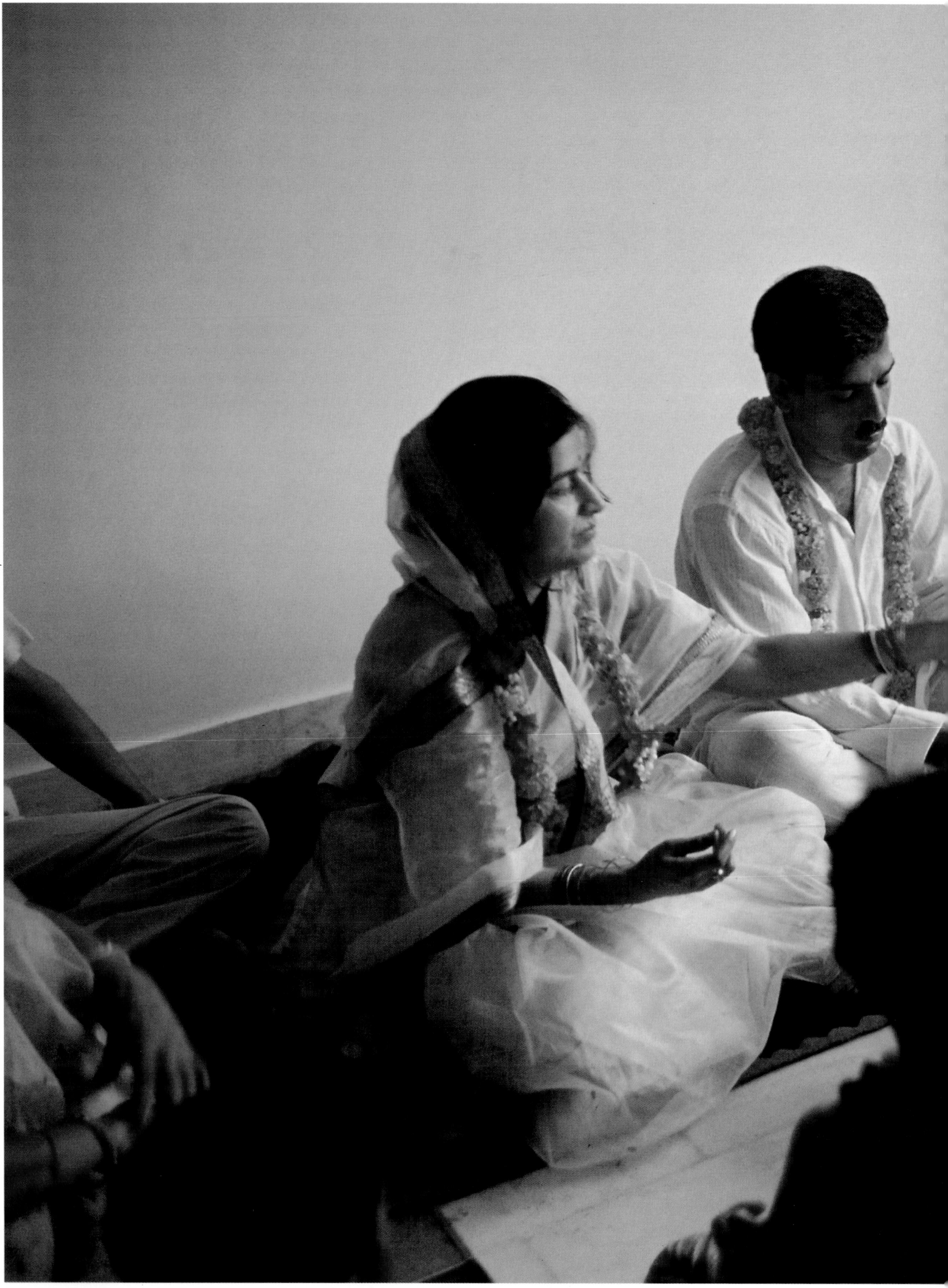

in household shrines or an elaborate temple ritual performed by priests according to guidelines laid down in non-Vedic texts such as the *Agamas* and Tantras. The ritual involves invoking the divine presence in an idol or an effigy of the divine; welcoming it with a bath; adorning it with flowers, incense, garments and jewellery; making offerings of food; entertaining it with music and dance; adoring it with lamps; saluting it; making petitions, and finally, bidding it farewell. During a typical puja, Shiva is offered raw milk and the leaves of the *bel* or wood apple; Vishnu and his incarnations are offered sweetmeats made of clarified butter, flowers and *tulsi*, or basil leaves; while the goddess receives bridal finery and neem or margosa leaves.

Samskaras are Vedic rites of passage. Rituals are held to mark important events in an individual's life: the naming ceremony; the first tonsure; the first time a child eats rice; the thread ceremony or initiation, mainly for Brahmin boys, after which they are allowed to read Vedic scriptures and perform Vedic rituals; the first day at school; marriage; childbirth, and finally, funeral rites. Of these, the naming ceremony, marriage and funeral rites are definitely observed by all.

While Hindus respect hermits, ideas of renunciation are not particularly encouraged in Hindu households. Marriage ensures entry into worldly life and is therefore considered a mandatory sacrament. It facilitates the rebirth of ancestors and ensures that the family line continues, especially if a son is born. During the ceremony, the bride and groom garland each other and exchange seven vows before relatives, the sacred fire, and the gods. They promise to share food, strength, wealth, happiness, progeny, cattle and devotion. The bride is adorned with the symbols of marriage: bangles, toe-rings, the necklace known as the *mangalasutra*, or auspicious thread, and red *sindoor* or vermilion powder in the parting of her hair. Bridal finery is considered auspicious and the adornment of the wife is said to bring luck to the husband and the household.

Vrata is the only ritual that does not involve priests. *Vrata* is observed on special days marked by the Hindu calendar and usually by women for the welfare of their families. It involves all-night vigils, fasting, food taboos, listening to stories of a particular god, drawing ritual diagrams, invoking gods by chanting their names or singing songs in their honour, visiting holy places, bathing in sacred rivers or tanks, making donations, and doing charitable deeds. A common *vrata* is the one in honour of Santoshi-ma, observed over sixteen Fridays. It involves abstaining from sour food, eating only once a day, lighting a lamp before her image, and listening to the Santoshi-ma *mahatmya* or the glory of the goddess who bestows satisfaction. Two other commonly observed *vratas* are the fast observed on Mondays by devotees of Shiva; and on *ekadashi,* the

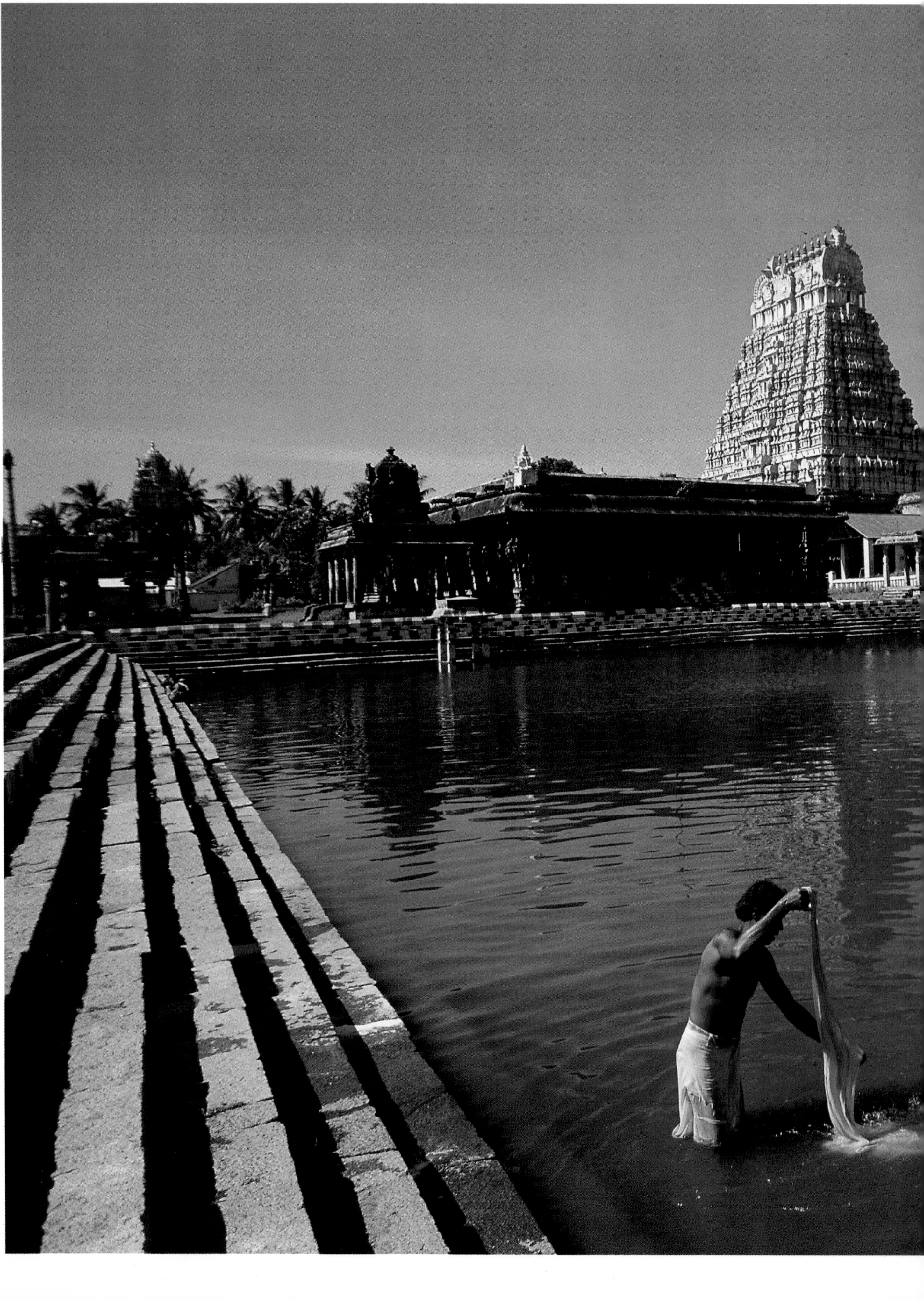

PAGES 62-63
The Devarajaswamy Temple, also known as the Varadarajar Temple, Kanchipuram, Tamil Nadu. In medieval times, these great temples were the heart of the life of a city. For many, a visit to the temple is still a part of daily life.

Below: *These ornamental spears at a rural shrine in Tamil Nadu sysmbolise guardian spirits.*
Facing page: *Such mendicants wander from temple to shrine, frequenting fairs and sacred cities, begging for alms along the way.*

eleventh day of the waxing or waning moon, by devotees of Vishnu. Some *vratas* are annual events like the Vat-Savitri when women circumambulate the banyan tree seven times, praying for the long life of their husbands. Other *vratas* performed by wives for the well-being of their husbands are Karva-Chauth in north India and Tiruvadira in south India.

Household rituals aimed at invoking benevolent cosmic forces are marked by the placement of auspicious symbols around the house. These include garlands of mango leaves and marigold flowers strung across the threshold; the drawing of sacred diagrams – known as *kolam* in the south, *alpana* in the east and *rangoli* in the north – at the entrance of the house, using coloured powder, rice flour, leaves and flowers; keeping pots filled with water and topped with a coconut placed on a mound of rice; distributing sweets; boiling milk until it overflows; lighting lamps and incense before images of gods; and painting a red swastika on the walls. The swastika is the ultimate auspicious symbol. The word is a derivative of *su asti*, which means, Let good things happen. Practices such as these ensure the prosperity of the household and peace within the family.

FESTIVALS AND PILGRIMAGES

The concept of a weekly day of rest does not exist in Hinduism. But there are numerous *utsavas* or festival days marked by rituals, merriment and no work. A festival may commemorate an astronomical event or a mythical occurrence, or celebrate a particular god. Some of the common Hindu festivals are Makara Sankranti, which marks the transition of the sun into Capricorn and the arrival of spring; Shivaratri, which celebrates the wedding of Shiva to the goddess Parvati; Rama Navami and Janmashtami, the birthdays of Rama and Krishna, respectively; Dussehra, which marks the goddess Durga's victory over the buffalo-demon, and Rama's victory over Ravana; and Diwali, when Lakshmi, goddess of good fortune, emerged from the ocean of milk.

A pilgrimage or *tirth-yatra* is an important Hindu practice to be undertaken at least once in a life. A journey to a sacred place, especially at an auspicious time, is said to wash away the effects of past misdeeds. On special days, fairs are held in sacred cities to welcome wandering hermits, travellers and pilgrims. The most popular of these fairs is the Kumbh Mela held in the cities of Allahabad, Haridwar, Nasik and Ujjain. A particularly auspicious Kumbh Mela occurs once in twelve years, in a cycle that is related to the movement of Jupiter. On this day millions of men and women seek to bathe in sacred waters, especially at the confluence of the Ganga and the Yamuna.

The place where a river originates, such as Nasik or Gomukh; or enters the plains, such as Haridwar; or merges with another river as in Allahabad, are all considered sacred. So are shrines atop mountain peaks such as Tirupati, where Vishnu resides as Venkateshwara. Cave shrines like Vaishno Devi and Amarnath are revered places of pilgrimage as are the sacred Hindu cities of Kashi or Varanasi, the city of Shiva; Puri, the city where Vishnu resides as Jagannath; Mathura and Dwaraka, the cities of Krishna; Ayodhya, the city of Rama; and Kanchipuram where the mother goddess is worshipped as Kamakshi. Himalayan shrines like Badrinath and Kedarnath, and temple cities such as Madurai in Tamil Nadu, are also popular places of pilgrimage.

THE HOLY COW

Since Vedic times, the cow has been the most revered animal in the Hindu world. Nothing is deemed to be worse than the killing of a cow. The greatest virtue is to take care of cows till the day they die a natural death. Cow's milk, dung and urine are common ingredients in rituals and ceremonies: they are believed to have purifying properties and the capacity to endow sacredness on everything they touch.

It is difficult to explain the sanctity bestowed on the cow. According to one theory, it is the direct result of the cow being the most valued commodity in Vedic times. Another theory finds the answer in allegorical symbolism. Vedic poets and metaphysicians used the cow as the metaphor for Nature. *Go Mata*, or Cow Mother, embodied the earth goddess whose udders nourished life on earth. Reverence for the cow is probably a ritualistic extension of reverence for Mother Nature.

Reverence for cows has also meant that beef is taboo in the Hindu diet. In fact, eating any kind of meat is considered polluting. Vegetarianism is an important and essential practice, especially amongst the devotees of Vishnu. But, like most things Hindu, this is not a universal practice.

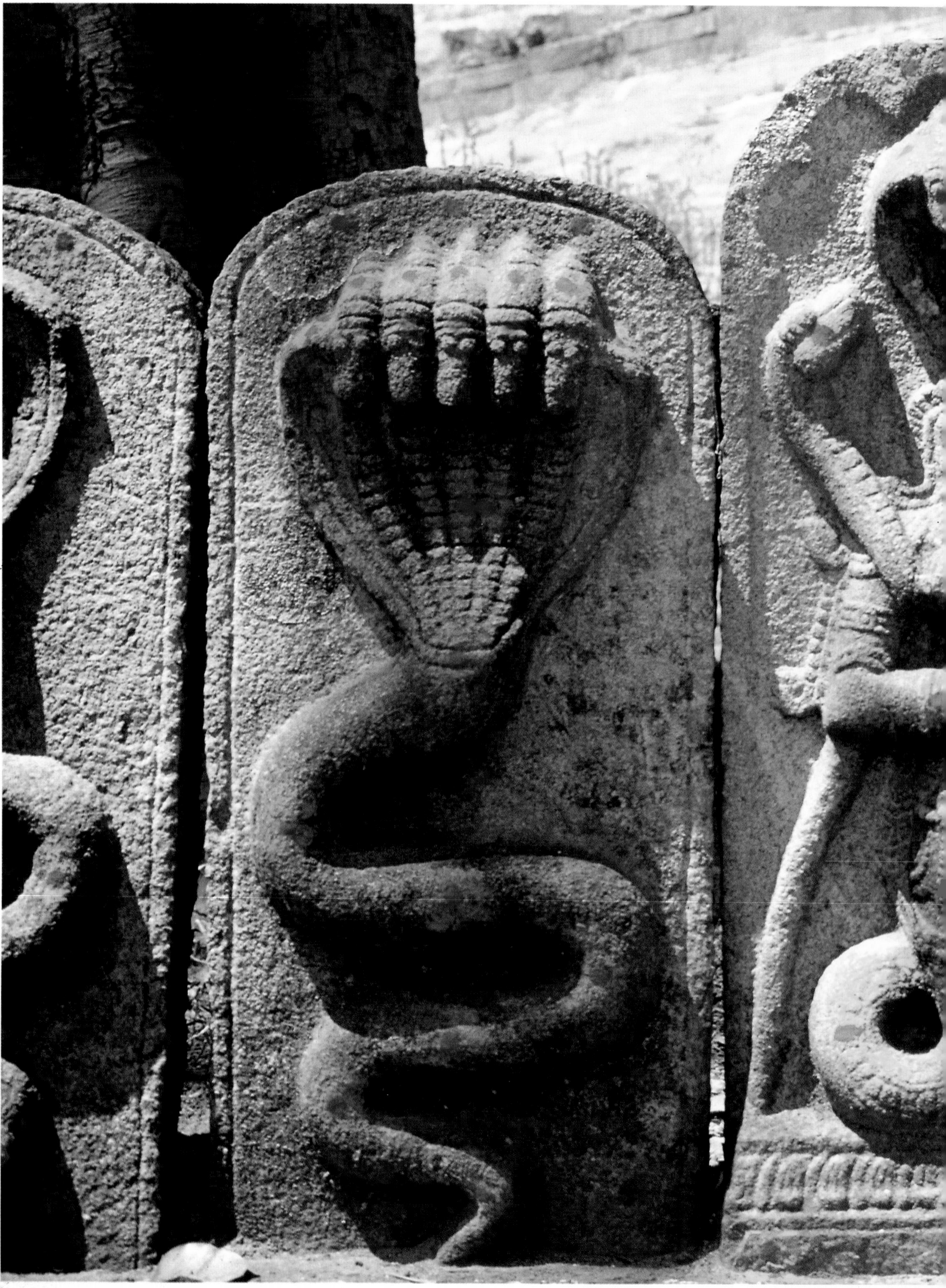

In some parts of India, blood-sacrifice and meat-eating are essential ingredients of goddess-worship. During the festivals of Dussehra and Diwali, male buffaloes, goats, rams and cocks are sacrificed to the mother goddess, manifest as the fierce Durga and the blood-thirsty Kali. Blood is said to restore the fertility of the earth goddess and calm her.

Offerings of blood, meat and alcohol are essential elements of non-Brahminical tantric rituals and most rural fertility rites. They are associated with devotees who are possessed by gods and goddesses. Besides restoring fertility, they are believed to appease the gods and ensure their benevolence.

THE TEMPLE: THE FOCAL POINT

The temple forms the focal point of Hindu life. Every house has a small shrine where images of personal and family gods are placed. Shrines can be seen everywhere: in vehicles, business establishments, fields, forests, on the wayside, beside rivers and atop hills. The most magnificent of these shrines are the grand temple complexes built in stone such as Ellora, Khajuraho, Konark, Tanjore, Halebid and Mahaballipuram, built between the eighth and fifteenth centuries.

The Hindu temple is not a communal prayer hall like a church or a mosque. It is the residence of a god or goddess. The patron deity of a temple can be symbolised by just a rock, or it can be an elaborately decorated idol of stone or metal. An idol has no special value until it is consecrated. Through a number of elaborate rituals, it is transformed into a container of divine aura. Devotees throng temples to get a darshan or glimpse of this manifestation of the divine.

During the darshan, the devotees absorb the grace of the deity and incorporate it into their secular lives. With constant exposure, the power of the idol gradually wanes until it is restored through rituals. To minimise the loss of its aura, the deity is isolated in the sanctum sanctorum, called the *garbha griha* or the womb room, which is rather dark, cramped and off limits to the public. Only priests who have been ritually cleansed are allowed to enter the room and touch the idol. However, once a year, the idol is taken out of the room and into the streets in a grand procession for the benefit of devotees.

Within the temple, darshan is allowed during special periods of the day and only for a brief period of time. During the darshan, devotees express their adoration, make offerings, present petitions, and seek divine blessings. Later, they collect the remains of all the ritual offerings (food, water, sandal paste, flowers, clothes), as these are supposed to transmit divine grace. Even the heat of the lamp that is waved before the idol is sought by all as it is considered a medium of the deity's aura.

The *garbha griha* forms the heart of the temple. Its roof is pyramidal in south Indian temples which follow the Dravida style, and curvilinear in north Indian Temples built in the Nagara style. A sacred pot and a flag are placed atop this roof. Around the central shrine is a vestibule through which devotees can circumambulate the shrine to express their devotion. In front is a hall of pillars where devotees gather for darshan. Often, a flight of stairs leads to this hall. The entire edifice, viewed as a celestial chariot, is usually built on a platform, shaped occasionally like a turtle or lotus.

Around the main shrine are smaller shrines of other gods and goddesses. There are also communal kitchens, marriage halls, dance halls and houses for hundreds of priests. High walls enclose the entire temple complex, and in south Indian temples, gateways known as *gopurams* are elaborately embellished with hundreds of images.

Scenes from myths and epics are often carved on temple walls. There are images of animals, plants, gods, demons, sages, courtesans, priests and warriors. Sex and violence are also graphically depicted. An attempt is thus made to capture all that exists in the cosmos and radiates out of the divine located at the heart of the shrine. The Hindu temple can therefore be seen as an architectural expression of Hindu metaphysics.

THE HINDU COSMOS

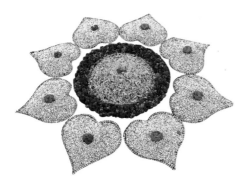

The ancients speculated on the origin of the universe and came up with many answers. According to the Vedas, the universe emerged when the Primal Being, Adi Purusha, was sacrificed and each portion of his body gave rise to a different world. In the *Upanishads*, the Primal Being split himself into the subject – the observer of life, and the object – that which is observed, and together, they set in motion the wheel of existence. According to the *Shiva Purana*, Shiva divided his body into male and female halves: from the former came spiritual reality and from the latter, material reality. In the *Vishnu Purana*, when Vishnu slept, the whole world became inactive but when he awoke, everything was activated: a lotus emerged from his navel on which sat Brahma who populated the world cradled in space and time.

SPACE: BRAHMA'S SPHERE

The Hindu cosmos is known as *Brahmanda* or Brahma's sphere. Everything is contained within it, even the divine. The *Brahavaivarta Purana* states: *Krishna created the world as an expression of his delight.* In this delightful world, are several worlds arranged vertically one on top of the other. From man's point of view these numberless worlds can be classified into three – the celestial realms or *lokas* wherein dwell the devas or gods and forefathers; the *talas* or nether regions wherein dwell nagas or serpents and asuras or demons; and *Bhu* or *Dhara*, the earth, inhabited by *manavas* or humans; *yakshas* and *ganas,* wild forest spirits; *rakshasas* or barbarians, and apsaras or river nymphs.

Right in the centre of *Brahmanda*, spanning the triple worlds is Mount Meru, the axis of space around which rotate the stars and planets. The continents radiate out of Meru like the petals of a lotus. Around the continents are seven concentric ocean rings, the salt-water ocean being the closest and the fresh-water ocean the farthest. In between are the oceans of treacle, wine, curd,

Pookkolam, *a floral decoration called Athapooru, is created in the front of every house in Kerala for ten days before Onam. A new colour of flower is added each day.*

butter and milk. Right on top of the cosmos is the highest heaven – the realm inhabited by those who have broken free from the cycle of rebirth. Devotees of Vishnu call this place Vaikuntha; devotees of Krishna call it Goloka, while devotees of Shiva call it Kailasa. It is the realm of absolute truth, of pure consciousness and perfect bliss.

These different realms have been interpreted as levels of awareness. At the lowest end are the materialistic creatures and at the highest, spiritual beings. Man is suspended in between, with the choice to climb up or tumble down.

VASTU: SCIENCE OF SPACE

Vastu is the Hindu occult science of space based on the belief that the different directions are under the influence of various gods, and a proper alignment of their powers ensures prosperity and averts tragedy. The table below identifies the *diggapalas*, divine guardians of directions.

North-West:	North	North-East
Vayu, wind-god	Kubera, god of wealth	Soma, moon-god
West	**Centre**	**East**
Varuna, sea-god	Brahma, the creator	Indra, rain-god
South-West	**South**	**South-East**
Surya, sun-god	Yama, god of death	Agni, fire-god

The *Vastu* Shastras are often consulted to make sure that a building does not violate the alignment of divine powers. Typically, all Hindu temples are east facing – east being the direction of Indra and all other gods. When a house faces south, an image of the mighty monkey-god, Hanuman, is often placed at the doorway to keep away Yama, the god of death, who rules the south. The north-east corner is considered especially auspicious as it is associated with Shiva in his Ishana form, bearing the moon on his head. This corner is associated with prosperity, power, affluence and abundance.

TIME: CYCLIC REPITITIONS

When Indra blinks, a man dies. When Brahma blinks, an Indra dies. When Vishnu blinks, a Brahma dies. When Shiva blinks, a Vishnu dies. Ideas such as these drive home the Hindu concept of time and put human lives in perspective.

The Hindu calendar, known as the *Panchanga*, measures time according to the rising and setting of the sun, the waxing and waning of the moon, and

Facing Page: H.H. Srikanthandatta Narasimbaraj Wodeyar, the Maharaja of Mysore, participates in the Dussehra procession for which the city is renowned.

Facing Page: Pandavani, a folk theatre form, involves the dramatic narration of the epics by a single actor, supported by a small chorus.

Below: *An image of Hindlaj Mata. This local deity at the Nagnechiji Temple, Jodhpur, is widely revered.*

the movement of the sun in solar and lunar houses. The year is divided into two halves: the auspicious half when the rising sun moves in the northerly direction, or *Uttarayan* – from the winter solstice to the summer solstice; and the inauspicious half or *Dakshinayana*. Within *Dakshinayana* are the *Chaturmaas,* four months of the monsoon when most festivities and pilgrimages are suspended. The year is also divided into six seasons: spring, summer, monsoon, autumn, early winter and late winter. There are twelve months in a year, each month characterised by the movement of the sun through one solar house and two and a half lunar houses. The day of twenty-four hours is divided arbitrarily into eight *praharas* or thirty *muhurats* or sixty *ghattikas*. Thus the *Panchanga* helps the Hindu plan his life.

Human life, however, is but a fraction of cosmic life. Just as humans die at the end of a lifespan to be reborn once more, the cosmos goes through cycles of birth and death. The death of the cosmos is known as *pralaya* or doom, when the earth spits fire and the oceans overflow until all that exists dissolves in the primal waters. Then, at the appropriate hour, the universe forms again and the cycle begins anew.

A single lifespan of the cosmos is known as *kalpa*. Each *kalpa* is divided into four eras or *yugas*. The first era is known as the *Krita Yuga*. It is the Golden Age when everything is perfect and the bull of dharma stands on all four limbs. Towards the end of the first *yuga*, the bull loses one of its legs and the second less-than-perfect age, the *Treta Yuga*, dawns. When the bull of dharma loses its second leg, the *Treta Yuga* comes to an end, and the *Dvapara Yuga* begins. This is followed by the *Kali Yuga*, the Dark Age, the present time, at the end of which the bull will lose its fourth leg and the flood of *pralaya* will sweep everything away.

In each *yuga*, Vishnu – in his role as preserver – walks the earth in a different form, sustaining order, ensuring that the march of time proceeds with predictable regularity. At the end of the *Krita Yuga* he is the warrior-sage Parashurama who slaughters the greedy kings of the earth; at the end of the *Treta Yuga* he is Rama, the king who establishes a perfect society at the cost of personal happiness; at the end of the *Dvapara Yuga* he is Krishna who teaches man to uphold dharma and live righteously in the midst of chaos and anarchy.

The Hindu world is thus like a cosmic merry-go-round spun through time. Everything that happens has happened before and will repeat itself in the future. No event is unique or spontaneous. No matter how hard one tries, the bull of dharma will lose its legs, the *yugas* will follow each other

and *pralaya* will overwhelm the world. The real purpose of life then is to break free from these repetitive phenomena, find meaning in them and through realisation, attain release.

ASTROLOGY: LUNAR READINGS

Jyotisha is Hindu astrology. It is considered a *vedanga*, a limb of the Veda that helps discern karmic patterns behind events. Unlike Western astrology, Hindu astrology is based on the actual position of the stars, and takes into account the fact that the position of the equinoxes with reference to the constellations is constantly changing. This occult science of time also focuses more on the *nakshatras,* lunar houses or asterisms, and less on the *rashi,* solar houses or zodiac. Central to *jyotisha* is the position of the nine celestial bodies or the *nava-graha* in the various solar and lunar houses. The *nava-graha* are: Surya, the Sun; Soma, the Moon; Mangal, or Mars; Buddha, or Mercury; Guru, also known as Brihaspati or Jupiter; Shukra, or Venus; Shani, or Saturn; and the nodes of the Moon, the bodiless Rahu and the headless Ketu.

When a child is born, parents immediately contact the astrologer and have the child's horoscope made based on the date, time and place of birth. Nowadays, computer software can generate this in minutes, though for interpretation and remedy, none but the family astrologer is trusted. The horoscope is regularly consulted to determine destiny, to forewarn against an imminent misfortune, and to help select a suitable spouse.

Jyotisha not only identifies planetary positions that cause misfortune but also offers remedial measures where applicable. Remedies include rituals to propitiate one of the nine celestial bodies. Images of the *nava-graha* are often enshrined in temples where devotees make offerings in the hope of offsetting their malevolence and attracting their benevolence. Special attention is given to Saturn and Mars which are commonly associated with misfortune. Offerings are also made to Hanuman, the monkey-god, who is said to have power over all celestial bodies and whose grace can override any astrological influence.

Wearing gemstones to enhance the power of a particular celestial body is another popular remedy. The gemstones prescribed are: ruby for the Sun, pearl for the Moon, red coral for Mars, emerald for Mercury, yellow sapphire for Jupiter, diamond for Venus, blue sapphire for Saturn, hessonite garnet for Rahu, and cat's eye or chrysoberyl for Ketu.

The astrologer has other duties besides reading horoscopes. Since he is familiar with planetary positions, he is often consulted to identify the *muhurat,* auspicious hour for a marriage, the inauguration of a business, or the start of a journey.

Facing Page: Pilgrims spread out their saris to dry at the Bikaneri dharamshala*, or pilgrims' rest house, in Haridwar.*

PAGE 82
Pilgrims take a ritual dip in a water tank near a temple.

The Hindu Being

It is said in the Veda: *As is the macrocosm, so is the mesocosm, and so is the microcosm.* Hence the word *purusha* refers simultaneously to the cosmic man, to the institution of society and to the human being. Hindu scriptures constantly stress that the universe ultimately rests within the individual: *What is without is actually within.* All things find their origin and final destination in the individual. Without the individual, the world does not exist. We are the seers, the observers. The world, as we see it, is the product of our perception and has no independent existence without us. This realisation transforms each and every one of us into creators, sustainers and destroyers of our own world, and enables us to realise the divine potential within ourselves. Hence the Vedic answer to the question of our true identity: *tat tvam asi* – you are that; *that* referring to the divine which pervades all things.

THE PHYSICAL, CONSCIOUS AND SUBCONSCIOUS

Jiva refers to a living being. Every *jiva* has an atman or soul, that is eternal, changeless, still and serene. The body is wrapped around the soul. According to the scriptures there are three types of bodies that wrap the soul: *sthula sharira* or gross body, *sookshm sharira* or subtle body, and *karana sharira* or causal body. These can be loosely and respectively identified with the physical body, the conscious mind and the subconscious mind, respectively. It is the causal body that is the repository of all memories, and karma that forces the soul to be dragged from one lifetime to another until the moment of liberation.

During the trauma of birth, the *jiva* loses touch with the causal body and the soul. Only through the practice of yoga is the connection reestablished. But to practice yoga, which involves mental discipline, *buddhi* or intellect is necessary to enable the *jiva* to make conscious choices, and not be entirely subject to instinct. Only humans have this faculty and this renders to human

Clusters of jasmine flowers bought by devotees as part of ritual offerings made to the deity during worship.

Facing Page: This half-submerged temple is a dramatic landmark along the ghats of Varanasi, which have structures dating to the medieval era.

birth a rare and golden opportunity to realise the divine and obtain release from the cycle of rebirths. Human birth is the result of good karma; if we squander it away we are doomed to go through several lifetimes as plants, animals, even minerals, until we earn enough merit to be born as humans again.

Yogis say that besides the intellect, the human mind has an ego that is the greatest obstacle to liberation. The ego is affected by internal cravings and external expectations. It fetters the mind and prevents it from becoming omniscient. Only when the ego is sublimated and the mind disciplined, can the intellect break the fetters of conditioning, realise truth and experience divinity.

The *Samkhya* texts state that the mind controls the body. The body is made up of five elements: earth, fire, water, wind and ether; it is composed of five sensory organs: the eyes, ears, nose, skin and tongue; and it has five organs of action: the face, hands, feet, genitals and anus.

In tantric texts, the subtle body or conscious mind is not restricted to the brain; it extends throughout the body. But this can be realised only through initiation and rigorous training under the guidance of a spiritual master. The aspirant unravels his true potential or kundalini, coiled like a serpent at the base of the spine. Through mantras or chants, yantra or charms, pranayama or breath manipulation, and asanas or exercises, he balances the solar and lunar forces of his body, the *Pingala* and Ida, or yang and yin, so that the central *Shushumna* channel is cleared of all obstacles. This enables the kundalini to uncoil itself and rise like a cobra through the spine, piercing the six chakras or centres of energy, entering the cranium and forcing the ultimate chakra to bloom like a thousand-petalled lotus in the head. These seven chakras known as *Muladhara, Svadhishthana, Manipura, Anahata, Vishuddha, Ajna* and *Sahasrapadma*, located at the base of the spine, genitals, navel, heart, throat, forehead and crown of the head, respectively, represent different levels of consciousness.

AYURVEDA AND YOGA

Ayurveda is the Hindu science of life and longevity. It is closely associated with the Atharva Veda, and is hence considered a gift of the gods.

Ayurveda cannot be isolated from Hindu metaphysics and the physiological principles of yoga and tantra. It views the body as the byproduct of the five elements: fire, water, earth, wind and ether; as a three-layered sheath comprising the flesh, the conscious and subconscious minds encasing the soul; as a collection of the seven tissues which are plasma, blood, fat, bone, marrow, nerves and reproductive tissues evolving

out of food; and as being under the influence of three humours – *vata, pitta* and *kapha* – translated loosely as wind, fire and water, respectively. Depending on which humour is dominant, one is said to possess either a *vata, pitta* or *kapha* constitution. The constitution determines health, predisposition to a particular methodology for staying fit, and therapies for combating disease.

Typically, a thin body frame, poor tissue development, a dry and cracked skin, the tendency towards a poor appetite, hard stools, scanty urination and intolerance of windy and dry weather characterise a *vata* constitution. People in this category tend to be restless, excitable and anxious. A *pitta* constitution is characterised by strong muscles, a warm and oily skin, ruddy complexion, sharp appetite, loose stools, profuse urination, and intolerance of heat and the sun. Such types are typically aggressive, dominating and prone to arguments. A person with a *kapha* constitution tends to be plump, with abundant tissue, moist skin, a large appetite, slow metabolism and intolerant of damp weather. Such a person tends to be calm, stable, loyal, possessive and sentimental.

People with a *vata* constitution are prone to sleep, nervous and joint disorders. Those with a *pitta* constitution are commonly afflicted by inflammatory conditions, infections, hyperacidity, skin rashes and liver problems. Respiratory and renal disorders are common in those with a *kapha* constitution.

When a disease strikes, Ayurveda helps the body get rid of toxins and generate energy to repair the damage. The treatment of an ailment can be constitutional or clinical. Constitutional remedies are for chronic ailments and include modification of diet, the intake of mild herbs, yoga and a proper lifestyle. Clinical remedies for acute illnesses involve reduction or removal of toxins, followed by tonification or rebuilding energy. Reduction includes a variety of practices such as consumption of strong herbs; fasting; massage with medicated oils; sweating therapy; yoga exercises; and the five cleansing practices of purgation, enema, vomiting, nasal medication and blood letting. Tonification involves the intake of a rich diet, tonics and strengthening herbs, adequate rest and relaxation, and the avoidance of excessive activity or stimulation.

86

Ayurveda is closely associated with yogic practices such as self-control, introspection, exercise, breath control, concentration and meditation. These practices seek to lead the mind away from *rajas,* states of agitation, or *tamas,* inertia, towards *sattva,* harmony. They affect both the subtle and the gross body and make it healthy so that the mind is strong enough to make its journey towards the divine.

THE AIM OF LIFE

When asked about the purpose of life is, the smriti texts unhesitatingly point to four goals that validate human existence: dharma or righteous conduct, *artha* or economic activities, *kama* or pleasurable pursuits, and moksha or the quest for liberation. There are shastras or manuals for each of these goals. Of these, the most fundamental and contentious is dharma. After all, what conduct is righteous?

Again the smriti texts come to the rescue. They state that action defined by varna or station in society, and ashrama – one's stage in life, is dharma. Varna-ashrama dharma forms the foundation of Hindu ideology.

Traditionally, there are four varnas or stations. The Rig Veda states that *purusha,* the personification of society, has for his head the Brahmins or priests and philosophers; for his arms the Kshatriyas or warriors and administrators; for his trunk the Vaishyas or farmers, herdsmen and traders; and for his feet, the Sudras or craftsmen and labourers. In time, the four varnas cascaded into hundreds of jatis or castes within a hierarchical system that gave more privileges to priests, noblemen and landed gentry, and very little to the labourers involved in 'unclean' professions which brought them in contact with animal hide, sewage, dirt and corpses. The latter came to be known as Untouchables, and the treatment meted out to them is one of the most shameful factors of Hinduism.

The word jati refers to a group of families who intermarry, dine only with each other, follow the same profession, have specific codes of conduct, and hold similar religious beliefs: Such is the hold of the caste system in India, that its rules are often retained even if individuals convert to Christianity or Islam.

According to the traditional view, no matter what one's jati, every human being has to go through the four ashramas or stages of life in order to validate his existence. These include the years as a *brahmachari,* a student preparing for life; and as a *grihasti,* householder, enjoying life and

fulfilling all social obligations. *Grihasti* is followed by *vanaprasthi* or retirement, making way for the next generation. The fourth and final stage is that of a sanyasi or hermit, working towards liberation.

For women, though, there is no varna or ashrama defining dharma. *Stri* dharma or righteous conduct for all women involves being a good daughter, sister, wife and mother. A woman who is the mistress of a prosperous house-hold, whose husband is alive and whose children are healthy, is called a *sowbhagyavati*, the lucky one, and *sumangali*, the auspicious one. Such a woman is often invited to participate in the joyous ceremonies of marriage, childbirth and fertility. Dressed in bridal finery, she is looked upon as a diminutive double of Lakshmi, goddess of abundance and good fortune.

Hinduism Today

That Hinduism does not have a single source or a standard doctrine has enabled it to acclamatise to change throughout history. Its most dramatic transformation was from the Vedic ritualism of the pre-Christian era to the bhakti ideology of the Christian era. Today, Hinduism continues to redefine itself to meet the needs of the modern man and woman who reject beliefs and practices based on ancient values, and medieval prejudices such as caste hierarchy and gender discrimination.

Hinduism is also affected by the fact that it is no longer confined to the Indian subcontinent. On the one hand, there are millions of Hindus now living in other countries, amidst other cultures, accommodating their religious inheritance with social realities. On the other, there are millions of non-Hindus who find in Hinduism the beliefs and practices which enable them to live a more fulfilling life.

Increasingly, there are many young people in India who do not go to temples or observe traditional rituals and festivals, but consider themselves Hindus nevertheless. There is a clear shift from practice to faith. Today, Hinduism is less about what one does and more about how one perceives life. To be a Hindu today, is to look at the world through a personal looking glass that is moulded by Hindu metaphysics and philosophy.

Facing Page: *A priest anoints a devotee at a wayside shrine dedicated to Lord Hanuman.*

PAGE 90
Lord Kumbeshwarar and his consort, Mangalambigaig, are brought to the Mahamakam tank, Kumba-konam, during the biggest bathing festival at a tank.

PAGE 91
Young boys dressed as Krishna during the Krishnaleela, Raghunath Temple, Imphal, Thanipur.

PAGES 92-93
The last journey. This is a common sight in Varanasi, where old people often come to die, for, according to belief, dying in Varanasi ensures liberation of the soul.

PAGES 94-95
Manikarni-ka-ghat, the great burning ghat of Varanasi where, it is said, the pyres have been burning continuously for the last 3000 years.

PAGE 96
A woman performing aarti.

89

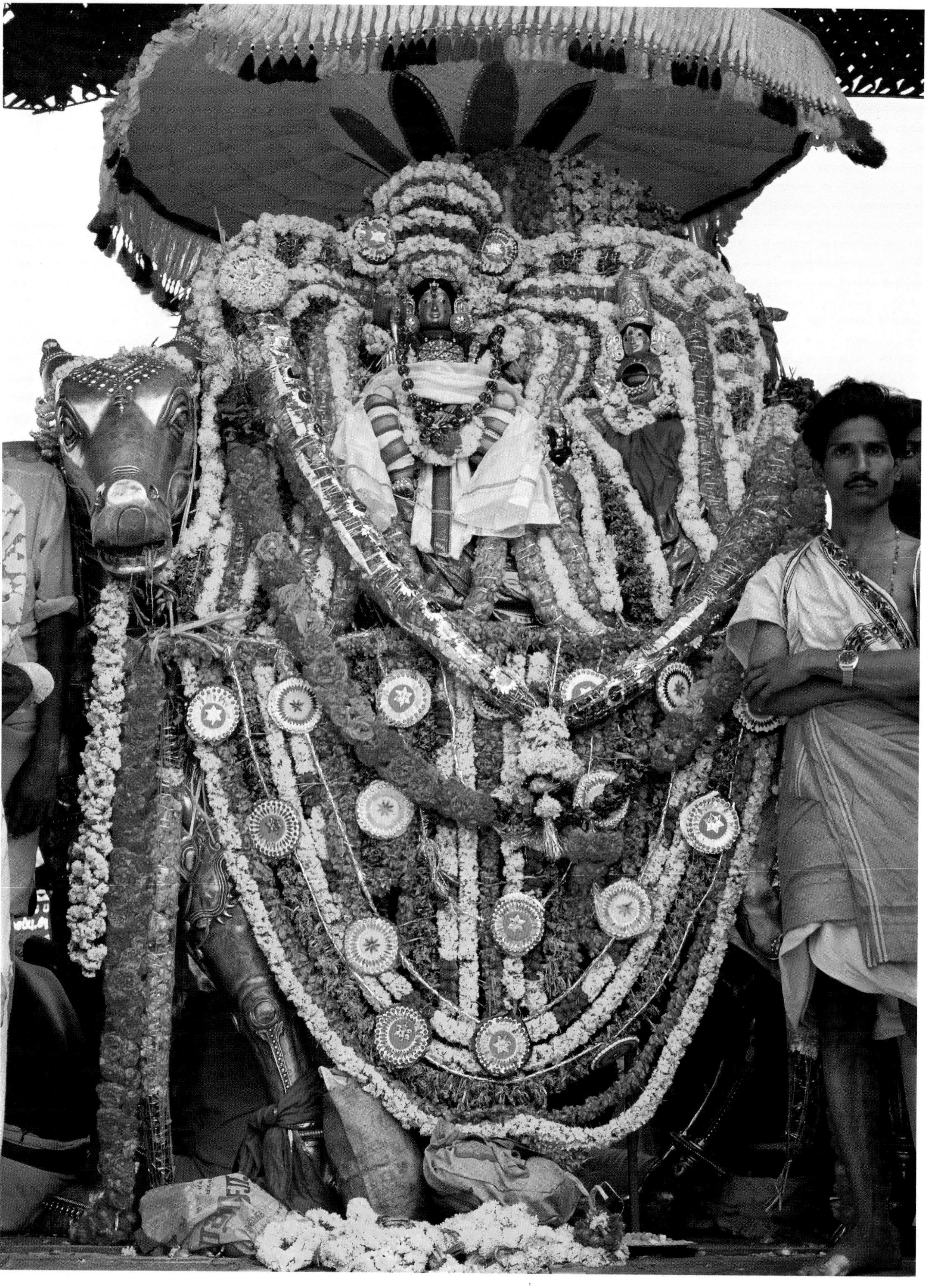

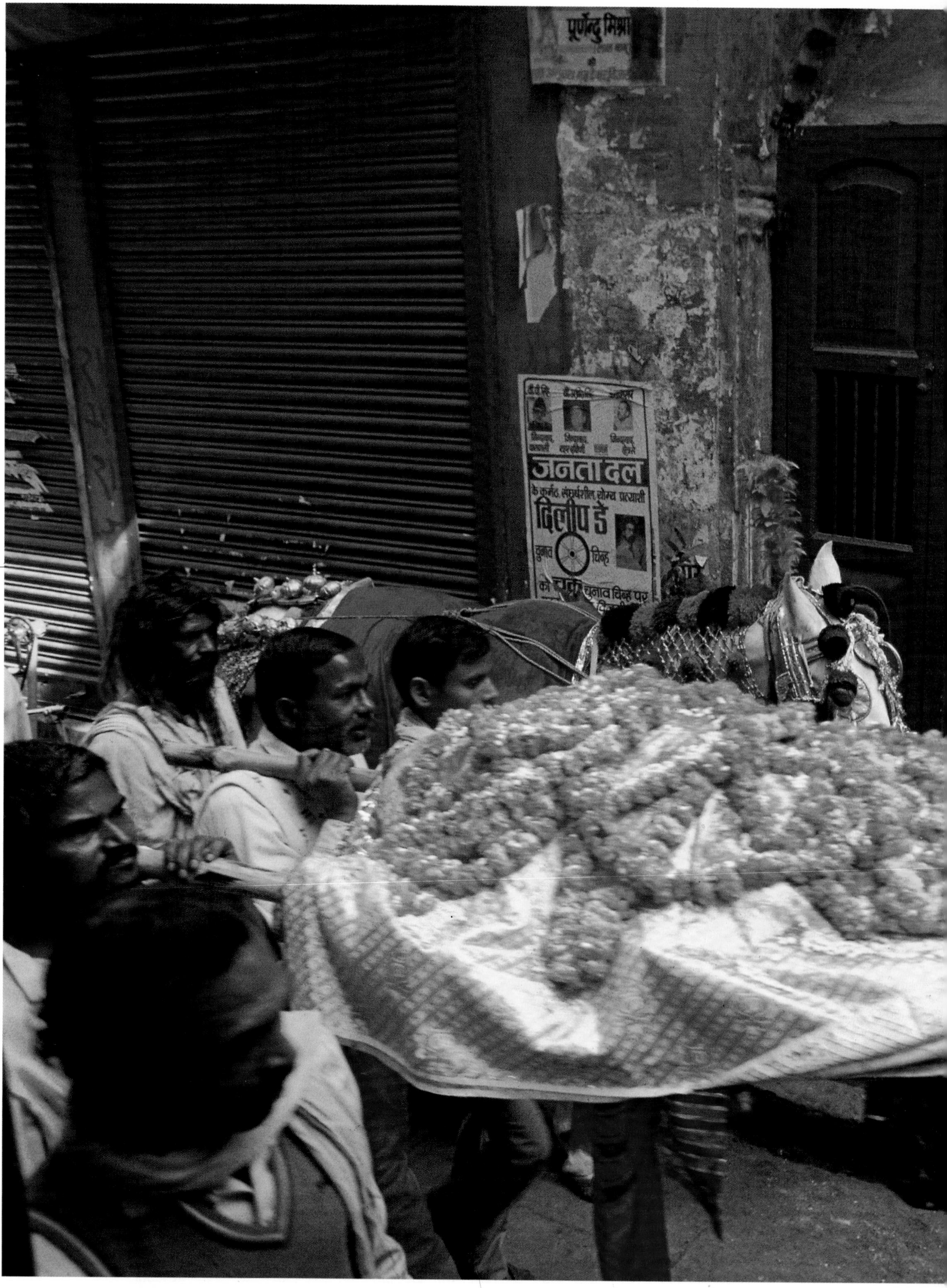
पूर्णेन्दु मिश्रा
जनता दल
दिलीप डे
चिन्ह
चुनाव चिन्ह पर

PHOTO CREDITS

Clare Arni, Aditya Arya, M. Balan, R. Fotomedia (Pvt.) Ltd., Phal S. Ghirota, V. Muthuraman, Avinasha Pasricha
Amit Pasricha, Aditya Patankar, Christine Pemberton, D. J. Ray, Sanjeev Saith
Shalini Saran, H. Satish, T. S. Satyan, Toby Sinclair
Amar Talwar, Dr. Bimla Verma, Henry Wilson